AF270657

SAN FRANCISCO 49ERS

KENNY ABDO

abdobooks.com

Published by Abdo Zoom, a division of ABDO, P.O. Box 398166, Minneapolis, Minnesota 55439. Copyright © 2022 by Abdo Consulting Group, Inc. International copyrights reserved in all countries. No part of this book may be reproduced in any form without written permission from the publisher. Fly!™ is a trademark and logo of Abdo Zoom.

Printed in the United States of America, North Mankato, Minnesota.
052021
092021

THIS BOOK CONTAINS RECYCLED MATERIALS

Photo Credits: AP Images, Getty Images, iStock, Shutterstock PREMIER
Production Contributors: Kenny Abdo, Jennie Forsberg, Grace Hansen
Design Contributors: Candice Keimig, Neil Klinepier

Library of Congress Control Number: 2020919709

Publisher's Cataloging-in-Publication Data

Names: Abdo, Kenny, author.
Title: San Francisco 49ers / by Kenny Abdo
Description: Minneapolis, Minnesota : Abdo Zoom, 2022 | Series: NFL teams |
    Includes online resources and index.
Identifiers: ISBN 9781098224783 (lib. bdg.) | ISBN 9781098225728 (ebook) |
    ISBN 9781098226190 (Read-to-Me ebook)
Subjects: LCSH: San Francisco 49ers (Football team)--Juvenile literature. | National
    Football League--Juvenile literature. | Football teams--Juvenile literature. |
    American football--Juvenile literature. | Professional sports--Juvenile literature.
Classification: DDC 796.33264--dc23

TABLE OF CONTENTS

SAN FRANCISCO 49ERS

Named after the 1849 gold miners of Northern California, the San Francisco 49ers are just as tough and determined as their namesakes.

As one of the National Football League's (NFL) older teams, the San Francisco 49ers have enjoyed great successes and many of the sport's most recognizable players.

KICK OFF

The San Francisco 49ers started
out in 1946. They were founded by
Tony Morabito. The 49ers were one
of the first teams in the All-America
Football Conference (AAFC).

In 1950, the 49ers joined the NFL.
Sadly, the team started off on the
wrong foot by losing their first game
to the New York Yanks 21-17.

During the 1960 season, coach Red Hickey and the 49ers became the first NFL team to use the shotgun formation. The **quarterback** receives the **snap** farther back from the **line of scrimmage**. It gives the **QB** more time to act.

TEAM RECAPS

Wide Receiver Dwight Clark made "the catch" in the 1981 **NFC** Championship game. It was a fingertip grab of a game-winning touchdown against the Cowboys.

The catch sent the 49ers to **Super Bowl** XVI, where they beat the Bengals 26-21!

Starting in 1985, the 49ers went on to win **Super Bowls** XIX, XXIII, and XXIV. The team struck gold again in 1995 with a record fifth win, beating the Chargers at Super Bowl XXIX!

GORDON
21
8

The 49ers once again made it to **Super Bowl** XLVII but lost to the Ravens 34–31. In the middle of the 2017 season, the 49ers got **quarterback** Jimmy Garoppolo in a trade with New England. He helped win five straight games by season's end.

The 49ers made it to **Super Bowl** LIV after an incredible 2019 season. It was their first appearance in seven years! Sadly, they lost to the Chiefs 31-20.

Many 49er players suffered injuries during the 2020 season, including Garoppolo. They ended with a 6-10 record. Middle linebacker Fred Warner was selected for the 2021 Pro Bowl and **AP All-Pros**!

HALL OF FAME

QB Joe Montana led the 49ers to four **Super Bowl** wins. He was named the game's **MVP** three times. During his time with the team, Montana had 35,124 passing yards. That is more than any other 49er.

Montana was **inducted** into the Pro
Football Hall of Fame in 2000.

Wide receiver Jerry Rice helped the team win three **Super Bowls**. When Rice retired from the NFL, he had 1,549 receptions and 197 receiving touchdowns! Rice was **inducted** into the Pro Football Hall of Fame in 2010.

PRO FOOTBALL
HALL OF FAME
CANTON, OHIO
NFL
ALUMNI
PRO FOOTBALL
HALL OF FAME
ENSHRINEE
PRO FOOTBALL
HALL OF FAME
CANTON, OHIO

Running back Frank Gore joined the 49ers in 2005. He rushed for more than 1,000 yards during eight different seasons. By 2013, Gore had rushed for over 11,000 total yards and 64 touchdowns. That is more than any other 49er.

29

GLOSSARY

AP All-Pro – an honor given by press organizations that names the best professional NFL players at each position during a season.

induct – to admit someone as a member of an organization.

line of scrimmage – the point on the football field where each play starts. It is a line that neither team can cross until the play has begun.

MVP – short for "most valuable player," an award given in sports to a player who has performed the best in a game or series.

National Football Conference (NFC) – one of two major conferences of the NFL. Each conference contains 16 teams split into four divisions. The winner of the NFC championship plays the AFC.

quarterback (QB) – the player on the offensive team that directs teammates in their play.

snap – passing the ball backwards to a teammate at the start of a play.

Super Bowl – the NFL championship game, played once a year.

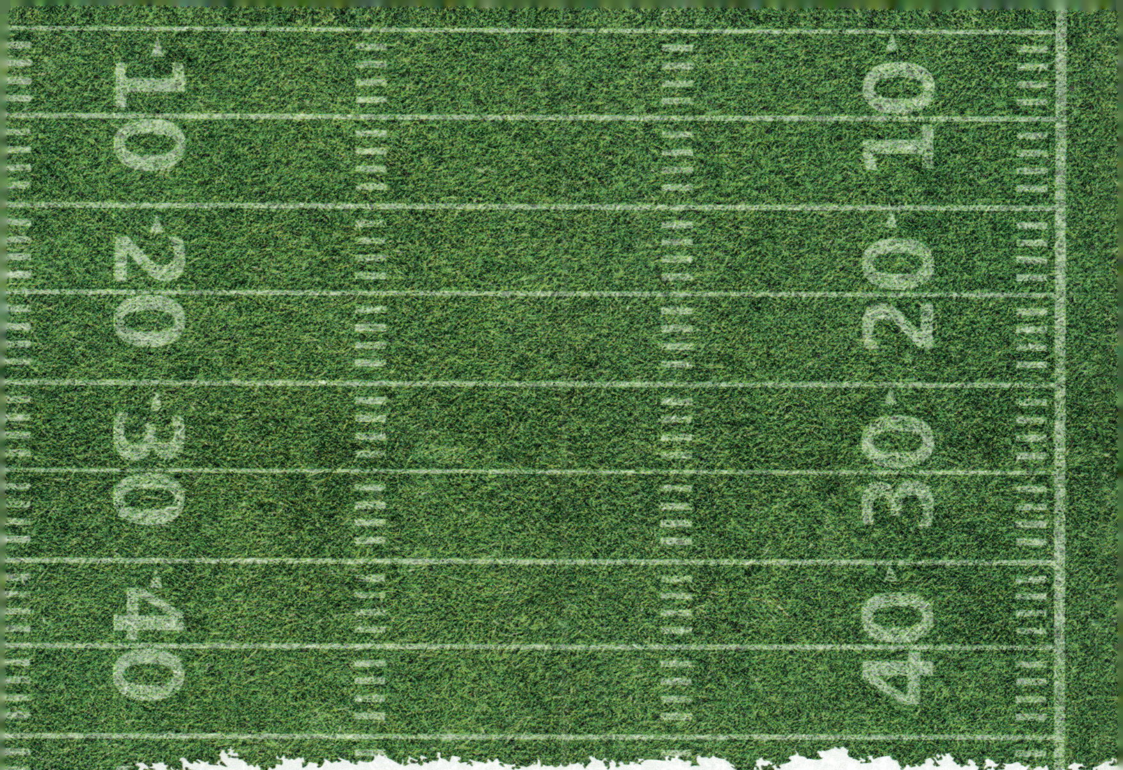

ONLINE RESOURCES

To learn more about the San Francisco 49ers, please visit abdobooklinks.com or scan this QR code. These links are routinely monitored and updated to provide the most current information available.

INDEX